ICE° KITCHEN

Poptails

CESAR & NADIA RODEN

50 SENSATIONALLY INTOXICATING COCKTAIL LOLLIES

Photography by Louise Hagger
Illustrations by Peter Roden

quadrille

CONTENTS

ICE°
KITCHEN

Our mission is to delight with new iced experiences. We have transformed the nostalgic classic childhood treat and turned it into a gourmet pleasure.

INTRODUCTION

High on lollies

There's something a little mischievous about turning a childhood treat into a strictly adult one. Our cocktail lollies, or "poptails", are a fun new culinary experience – delicious, elegant, luxurious, playful and quirky.

The idea for this book came about while I was experimenting with flavours and randomly dipped a watermelon ice lolly into a glass of rum to see how the flavours matched. While sucking the alcohol off the frozen lolly, I realized that this was something so special that I called Cesar right away to tell him how great it was. He laughed because I told him I had to pick my daughter up from school slightly tipsy. It planted a seed that led to the creation of this book, and the dipping into a well-matched alcohol became an important aspect of many of the recipes.

One thing led to another...

At Ice Kitchen, we are continually finding ways to delight in ice. While Cesar runs the production kitchen in London, I run the experimental kitchen in New York. We Skype almost every day to discuss flavours and ideas.

We have both toyed with the notion of a poptail bar serving our alcoholic concoctions, which we like to see as pop art. I am not a heavy drinker, but I find the flavours and history of mixed drinks very creative and imaginative, and the pairing of drinks to other ingredients felt like exciting new territory. Cesar, on the other hand, enjoys the clubs, bars and social drinking culture of London. The floodgates opened.

The experiments

I love experimenting, putting together ingredients that complement each other. I start with one and add another, getting a delicate balance of flavours that enhance each other or create an unexpected clash. Sometimes this clash leads to another "story" altogether, like the Figs Go South of the Border poptail (page 64) with Mediterranean flavours meeting in Mexico. When I wrote the original draft for this book I found that I had written the expression "the so-and-so flavour shines through" in almost every recipe. I laughed at myself for writing the sentence so many times, but the point I was trying to make was that each flavour needs to express itself distinctly, like notes in a piece of music.

Alcohol doesn't like to freeze

The fact that alcohol doesn't like to freeze was a challenge – but this led to some unexpected and delicious solutions, such as using raisins or bits of fruit soaked in alcohol in the mixtures, and finding the alcohols that had stronger, more distinctive tastes, so that the flavour gave the feeling of alcohol when the content was low. But most of all, it led to the idea of dipping the poptails into a glass of well-matched alcohol, and this became a big part of the excitement.

The lore of cocktails and magic at the table

I have become fascinated with the whole lore of cocktails, the stories and rituals and the romance behind them, and have fallen in love with the bottles themselves – the way their intriguing shapes and labels reflect the era in which they were first commercially introduced. I have learned all kinds of things – for instance that the bartender at the Hôtel Ritz in Paris, Frank Meier, was also a spy for the French Resistance.

The ceremony and presentation around enjoying a cocktail establish a mood, and set aside time to please yourself and your guests. Each poptail becomes a still life at the table, a little story that takes you elsewhere – the Pommes-Pommes poptail (page 82) with the red rose puts you right at the Paris Ritz, the Tequila Sunrise (page 40) with its lipgloss-red glacé cherry puts you on the Rolling Stones Tour in 1972, Napoleon's Retreat (page 78) takes you to 19th-century France. The stories and naming of the poptails give them meaning and humour – the one for "real men" makes me laugh every time.

The rolling, swirling or dipping of the poptails into exciting garnishes came from the idea of the traditional pairing of cocktails with bar snacks and it led to some fun combinations, like the Chocolate Chilli Whisky Swizzles (page 98) dipped into crispy bacon pieces, or the Bourbon Vanilla (page 102) rolled into smashed crunchy amaretti.

The poptails are highly coloured and gem-like, and the garnishes – suspended fruits, cut zests, berries pierced with cocktail sticks, with umbrellas and miniature toys – all add to the excitement, drama and sense of fun.

Home with blurred sensibilities

The kitchen where I experiment in my loft in SoHo, New York is attached to my art studio. I live there with my eight-year-old daughter Lily. Due to demolition and construction work in my building, I haven't had any gas for over nine months, and have only a little hot plate and tiny toaster oven to cook with. But this hasn't stopped my kitchen from turning into an inebriated Ice Kitchen laboratory, with the whole kitchen counter becoming a drinks cabinet. Friends popping in and visitors coming to see my artwork would end up with fistfuls of poptails to comment on and as many shot glasses to dip them into, thus blurring their artistic sensibilities.

Lion's Milk and more...

Cesar and I have been in contact with bartenders, trying to collect secrets and customer favourites. I have updated old lost cocktails and frozen their components, deconstructed others and created twists on classics, and concocted new combinations from our own stories and experiences. The Lion's Milk (page 62) with arak, yogurt and honey is inspired by my grandfather Cesar's – who is Cesar's great-grandfather – regular drink with a mezze. The Zabaglione (page 116) recalls something my mother Claudia gave me every afternoon as a child. Some poptails evoke a bygone era, some recall memorable times and places – a bar in London, a magical garden party in New York, a street in Sorrento in Italy, a terrace café in Paris. The most indulgent, the Grand Marnier Custard & Raspberries (page 108), evolved from a special Christmas lolly commissioned by Claridge's, and it holds a little culinary secret. You'll find many spritzes and an obsession with all things Negroni – there would have been more than three Negroni poptails if there had been more room!

Now we invite you into the world of Ice Kitchen poptails... Let the party begin!

Nadia Roden

THE
TECHNIQUES

NUTS & BOLTS OF A POPTAIL

1. Poptails are often dipped or rolled into a small glass or plate of well-matched alcohol.

2. Garnishes add to the drama and fun, and can highlight flavours in the poptail. They should be treated with the same formal presentation as if they were a cocktail.

3. Something sprinkled on can add another layer of texture.

4. You must be careful not to put too much alcohol in the mix, or it will remain slushy. Do not exceed the amount stated in the recipes.

5. Poptails can be icy and light or rich and creamy.

6. Lemons and limes are an important ingredient in most poptails; they contrast with the sweet element and liven up the flavour. Always use freshly squeezed lemon or lime juice.

7. Because fruits vary so much in sweetness and ripeness, always taste and adjust the sugar if necessary, remembering that the mixture will taste less sweet when frozen.

8. Use the best-tasting alcohols, because they mysteriously strengthen in taste when frozen.

You'll have people waiting for poptail hour!

TOOLS

Kitchen scales

Food processor or **blender**
to purée and mix fruit

Board and **knife**

Mixing bowl

Measuring spoons
and **measuring cups**

Transparent measuring jug
with very small increments to
measure alcohol and larger
increments for the mixtures

Small or **medium saucepan**
to make simple syrups, cook
fruit or heat milk

Good juicer (e.g. electric)
for juicing oranges, lemons
and grapefruits

Heatproof spatula
for scraping syrups out of
saucepans, stirring a mixture
over heat or through a sieve

Fine zester for zesting
citrus peel

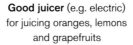

Fine-mesh sieve to strain
out solids, such as spices
and seeds

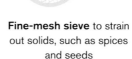

Lolly sticks
(page 18)

Ice lolly moulds
(page 18)

Glasses
for dipping into and for use
as moulds (page 18)

EXPERIMENT WITH MOULDS

There are many ready-made regular plastic ice lolly moulds to choose from, in many shapes and sizes. It is best to use slimmer, smaller moulds because they fit easily into a glass for dipping. Here are some other ideas that work well.

1. Shot glasses
These are perfect for poptails; you can even serve them straight from the shot glass. Remember that the bottom can never be wider than the top, or the poptail will not come out.

2. Silicone moulds
These work really well because they are so flexible that the poptail can be removed easily and immediately. There are not many silicone ice-pop moulds, but there are small silicone baking moulds that work perfectly for poptails.

3. Metal or kulfi moulds
These are hard to find, but work well because it's easy to remove the poptail from them.

4. Tiny wax-lined paper cups
These are especially good if you need to make many for a large party. Make sure they are lined with wax, otherwise the poptails won't come out easily. You can also use plastic ones.

5. Ice cube trays
A great option for when you want a quantity of bite-sized poptails. You can use cocktail sticks or twigs as sticks. Silicone ice cube trays work especially well because you can pop them out so easily.

BE PLAYFUL WITH STICKS

Traditional wooden lolly sticks are easy to find and work so well, but you can also be playful. For positioning the sticks, let the mixture freeze to slush before inserting (as described on page 22).

Here are some possibilities:

1. Traditional lolly sticks
2. Twigs with leaves
3. Cocktail swizzle sticks
4. Coffee spoons
5. Chopsticks
6. Wooden cocktail sticks and bamboo skewers
7. Hard decorative paper straws (cut small)
8. Light glow sticks

ALCOHOL

Since alcohol freezes at a much lower temperature than water, be careful not to put too much in or the poptails will become slushy and break apart when you try to unmould them. Use just a little – do not exceed the amount stated in the recipes – so that the alcohol stays suspended around the other frozen ingredients.

The key is to use stronger-flavoured alcohols, so the taste is there even when the quantity is low. The flavour of alcohol is also heightened when frozen. For an extra punch, you can soak fruit, such as raisins or pieces of apple, strawberry or orange, in alcohol before adding them to the poptail mix; the alcohol bursts out as you bite into the fruits. The best idea of all is to dip the poptails into a small glass of well-matched alcohol.

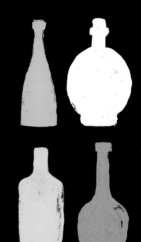

GARNISHES

Garnishes give the poptails a sense of theatrics; they can also highlight or contrast a particular taste. Arrange them as if it were a cocktail.

1. Fruit pieces spiked through a cocktail stick (look at the Tequila Sunrise and Blackberry Bramble on pages 40 and 66).

2. A fruit slice can help support a stick while freezing the poptail.

3. An artfully positioned piece of zest adds panache.

4. A miniature umbrella or toy can be fun and take you "somewhere else".

5. Make patterns out of fruits and berries on the serving plate or tray. It's also fun to create an environment (look at the Blue Lagoon on page 52).

6. Suspend a fruit slice or herb above or in the poptail mixture.

7. For a little surprise, skewer an alcohol-soaked strawberry, raspberry, cherry or chunk of pineapple onto the lolly stick before inserting it into the mould.

8. To layer flavours, freeze the first one for about an hour, then add the next, adding the stick after the first or second layer.

DIPPING, DRIZZLING & ROLLING

1. Dipping the poptail into a shot glass of well-matched alcohol is delicious – you only need a small amount of alcohol to set off the poptail. Use slim moulds so that the pop fits into the glass. Suck the alcohol off and dip again.

2. You can swirl and twirl the poptails into the chosen alcohol – for spritzes, a larger glass works well.

3. You can serve a poptail on a plate that is drizzled with alcohol – roll it in the alcohol as you eat it. You can also lay the poptail in a small bowl and drizzle more alcohol over it.

4. For extra texture and complementary flavour, sprinkle crumbled garnishes on individual plates, or in a dipping bowl, and roll your pops into the crumbs as you eat. Make sure the pop is moist with alcohol so that the crumbs stick. The matches are endless: sweet shredded coconut, crumbled crispy bacon, amaretti or vanilla wafers, smashed nuts, spices, seeds or chocolate.

SERVING SUGGESTIONS

You have to work fast when serving poptails so that they don't melt before you present them. Serve them in place of a cocktail, or at the end of a dinner party with the dessert, or as the dessert itself. Some work well as a palate cleanser between courses, or as canapés for a special occasion. If there are lots of people, it's a nice idea to serve a variety of small ones at intervals, to avoid them melting.

You can serve poptails on their own or with a small glass of alcohol for dipping, passing them round on a tray over ice, or individually on a plate drizzled with a special liqueur. You can roll them in crumbs and garnish, and they can be served unmoulded in shot glasses, or presented on a plate over a pattern of fruit slices. If you don't mind sharing, you can serve them around a communal dipping bowl of alcohol or garnishes.

You can enjoy a poptail at any time of day, but here are some suggestions:

Lazy afternoon
Lychee Martini (page 92), Mango Margarita (page 96), Campari Orange (page 28), Pineapple Pastis (page 56), The Existentialist (page 90), Amaretto Peach (page 60)

Dinner party
Kahlúa Coffee Pops (page 110), Zabaglione (page 116), Chocolate Negroni (page 100), Sauternes Almond & Orange Blossom Dream (page 120), Bourbon Vanilla (page 102), Figs Go South of the Border (page 64), Raspberry Limoncello (page 30), Tango Bravo Whisky (page 58), Port & Poached Pear (page 118)

Indulgent pleasure
Grand Marnier Custard & Raspberries (page 108), Chocolate Negroni (page 100), Orange Liqueur Creamsicles (page 106), Piña Colada (page 42)

Garden party, barbecue or wedding
Rosé with Strawberries & Basil (page 72), Mixed Berries in Riesling (page 70), Pimm's on a Stick (page 86), La Paloma (page 38), Aperol Orange Tarragon Spritz (page 74), Flower Garden (page 88)

Romantic evening or rooftop party
Strawberry Daiquiri (page 34), Pink Negroni (page 26)

Inebriated dinner party
Blue Lagoon (page 52), Dark & Stormy Mojito (page 36), Watermelon Margarita (page 32)

Brunch party
Bloody Mary (page 124), Napoleon's Retreat (page 78), Orange & Blossom Mimosa (page 80), Pommes-Pommes (page 82), Peach Bellini (page 84), Blackberry Bramble (page 66)

Festive season
Eggnog (page 114), Rum Raisin (page 104), Royal Red Cranberry Spritz (page 76)

THE PROCEDURE

1. Fill the moulds

Pour the poptail mix into the moulds from a small jug or measuring cup. If there are pieces to suspend, make sure you distribute them evenly. If you want to insert a garnish, such as a sliver of orange or lemon, or a mint leaf, then now would be the time to do it. Leave a 5-mm/¼-in gap at the top for expansion during freezing.

2. Freeze

Turn your freezer to the coldest setting and clear a flat surface to put the moulds on. Prepare ahead, allow for plenty of freezing time and avoid opening the freezer often. Poptails take longer to freeze because of the alcohol content – about 5–8 hours depending on size and alcohol content. Freezing overnight is best.

3. Tie a string on your finger

Don't forget that you'll need to insert the sticks in a little while!

4. Insert the sticks

The easiest method is to leave the moulds uncovered and to insert the sticks after the mixture has frozen enough that the sticks stay straight when inserted, about 60–90 minutes. But don't forget to put the sticks in! Another idea is to secure them in place with a sliced piece of fruit (page 19). If your timings don't fit, you can cover the top of your moulds with foil and cut little slits where you will want the sticks, then insert the sticks through the foil; it will secure them in place.

5. Unmould

You have to take care when unmoulding poptails because the alcohol in them makes them more delicate. Metal or rubbery silicone moulds work best. With the latter, all you need to do is push them out. For other types of mould, you can leave the poptails sitting at room temperature for a few minutes or dip them in room temperature water for a few seconds as you pull gently on the stick. If the mould is a shot glass, hold it in your hands until you are able to pull the poptail out. Twisting the stick a little as you pull will make them come out more easily. If the poptail melts too much, the stick will come out without the pop.

6. Storing

Keep the poptails in their moulds as long as possible to prevent freezer burn. It is best to serve poptails as soon as possible after unmoulding, but if you need to store them, wrap them individually in cling film (plastic wrap) and store in the freezer in an airtight freezer bag. They taste best within a week of making.

1.

2.

3.
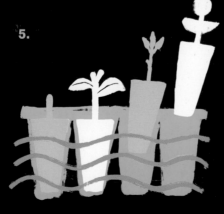

4.

5.

6.

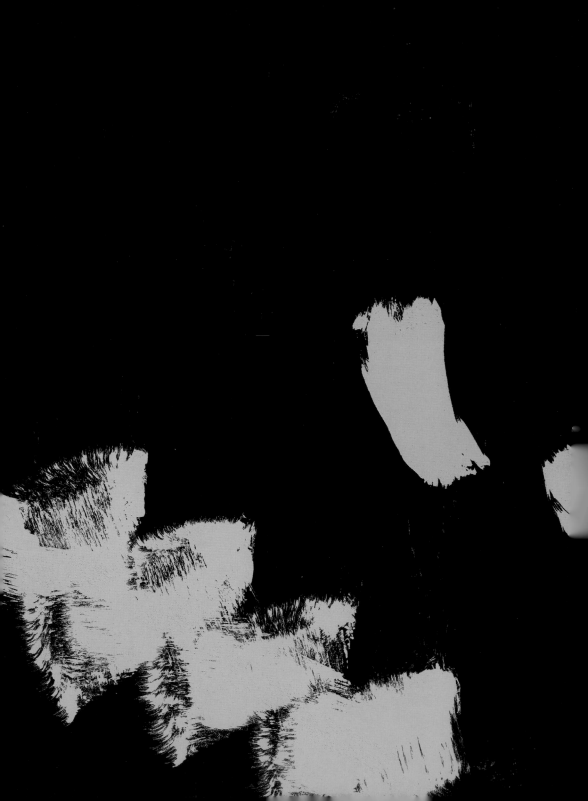

THE POPTAILS

PINK NEGRONI

Ruby grapefruit, Campari, gin

Makes 8–10

It is said that on his return from England in 1919, an Italian nobleman, Count Camillo Negroni, asked his favourite bar to prepare his usual cocktail, the Americano, but with a splash of gin instead of the usual soda. The bittersweet combination became a classic. In these delicious pink poptails, a family favourite, the grapefruit takes the place of the traditional sweet vermouth, adding zest. They are delicious on their own, and super dipped in a shot glass of gin.

120ml/½ cup water
110g/½ cup granulated sugar
600ml/2½ cups freshly squeezed ruby grapefruit juice (from about 3–4 grapefruits)
75ml/5 tablespoons Campari
3 tablespoons gin

For the garnish (optional):
sliver of grapefruit or a mint leaf for each

Put the water and sugar in a small saucepan and gently heat until the sugar has dissolved. Mix together with the grapefruit juice, Campari and gin.

Fill the moulds, leaving a little space at the top. If you like, put a sliver of grapefruit or mint leaf into the top of each.

Freeze until slushy, 60–90 minutes, then insert the sticks and freeze until solid, at least 5 hours or overnight. (See page 22 for the complete procedure.)

CAMPARI ORANGE

Orange, Campari, lime

Makes 8–10

The bittersweet combination of Campari and orange comes from the 1960s. It was originally named after the Italian hero Garibaldi, whose uniform colour resembled that of the cocktail. He had fought for the unification of Italy, and the cocktail represents that unification: the Campari from Milan and the oranges from Sicily. It's one of our favourites.

The recipe for Campari has been a closely guarded secret for more than 150 years. We know it's made by infusing herbs and fruit in alcohol and water, and that the distinctive red colour was once derived from ground-up scales of cochineal insects – but you'll be relieved to hear that's not in the recipe any more.

60ml/¼ cup water
110g/½ cup granulated sugar
600ml/2½ cups freshly squeezed orange juice (from about 6–7 oranges)
80ml/⅓ cup freshly squeezed lime juice (from about 3–4 limes)
90ml/6 tablespoons Campari

For the garnish (optional):
sliver of orange for each

Put the water and sugar in a small saucepan and gently heat until the sugar has dissolved. Mix together with the orange juice, lime juice and Campari.

Fill the moulds, leaving a little space at the top. If you like, put a sliver of orange into the top of each.

Freeze until slushy, 60–90 minutes, then insert the sticks and freeze until solid, at least 5 hours or overnight. (See page 22 for the complete procedure.)

RASPBERRY LIMONCELLO

Raspberries, limoncello, lemon

Makes 8–10

Limoncello liqueur is made from steeping lemon zest in spirit until the oils are released. When I make this poptail I'm reminded of the time I danced at night with friends in the streets of Sorrento to the music of Renato Carosone. These poptails are perfect on their own, but you can also dip them into a shot glass of pure limoncello. Don't strain out the raspberry seeds; the crunch adds to the experience.

300g/2½ cups raspberries
100ml/⅓ cup limoncello, plus extra, optional, for dipping
140g/⅔ cup caster or granulated sugar
150ml/⅔ cup freshly squeezed lemon juice (from about 3–4 lemons)
300ml/1¼ cups water

For the garnish (optional):
sliver of lemon for each

Put the raspberries in a bowl, stir in the limoncello and sugar and set aside to macerate for at least 15 minutes.

Transfer to a food processor, add the lemon juice and water and blend until smooth. Fill the moulds, leaving a little space at the top. If you like, put a sliver of lemon into the top of each.

Freeze until slushy, 60–90 minutes, then insert the sticks and freeze until solid, at least 5 hours or overnight. (See page 22 for the complete procedure.)

WATERMELON MARGARITA

Watermelon, lime, tequila, triple sec

Makes 8–10

Everybody has been fighting over who came up with the Margarita. My favourite story is that Don Carlos Orozco, a bartender in Mexico, had been experimenting with drinks when Margarita Henkel, the daughter of a German ambassador, walked in. First to test his concoction, it was in her honour that he christened it. This watermelon variation is extra refreshing. For the full monty, dip it in a shot glass of tequila and keep dipping.

60ml/¼ cup water
65g/⅓ cup granulated sugar
650g/4 cups watermelon chunks
90ml/6 tablespoons freshly squeezed lime juice (from about 2–3 limes)
60ml/¼ cup tequila, plus extra, optional, for dipping
2 tablespoons triple sec (orange liqueur)

For the garnish:
thin slice of lime for each

Put the water and sugar in a small saucepan and gently heat until the sugar has dissolved. Remove from the heat and allow the syrup to cool for a few minutes.

Put the watermelon and syrup in a food processor and blend until smooth. Strain the mixture through a sieve into a bowl, stirring it with a spoon and pressing it through, until just the seeds are left in the sieve. Stir in the lime juice, tequila and triple sec.

Fill the moulds, leaving a little space at the top. Push the lolly sticks though a thin slice of lime and insert them into the moulds; the lime slice secures the stick.

Freeze until solid, at least 5 hours or overnight. (See page 22 for the complete procedure.)

STRAWBERRY DAIQUIRI

Strawberries, rum, lime

Makes 8–10

The Daiquiri, a drink associated with summer, was invented by an American mining engineer, Jennings Cox, who was in Cuba at the time of the Spanish-American war. Try serving this poptail on a small plate and trickling rum over it. Ernest Hemingway – a Daiquiri imbiber – would approve.

450g/1lb strawberries, hulled and quartered
100g/½ cup caster or granulated sugar
2 tablespoons freshly squeezed lime juice
90ml/6 tablespoons white rum, plus extra, optional, for trickling
125ml/½ cup water

For the garnish (optional):
thin slice of strawberry for each

Put the quartered strawberries into a bowl, sprinkle over the sugar, stir in the lime juice and rum and set aside to macerate for 30 minutes, or longer.

Transfer to a food processor, add the water and blend until smooth.

Fill the moulds, leaving a little space at the top. You can push the lolly sticks though a thin slice of strawberry if you like and insert them into the moulds; the strawberry slice will secure the stick. (Alternatively, freeze until slushy, 60–90 minutes, then insert the sticks.)

Freeze until solid, at least 5 hours or overnight. (See page 22 for the complete procedure.)

DARK & STORMY MOJITO

Hibiscus, ginger, lime, rum

Makes about 15 small

Here, our made-up Mojito is a Jamaican twist on the "Dark & Stormy"
cocktail. The spicy mix of hibiscus, ginger, lime and rum creates a poptail
that conjures up tropical heat; in Jamaica, they often pair red hibiscus with
ginger. These poptails are intense, so make them in small moulds. Dipping
them in rum is optional.

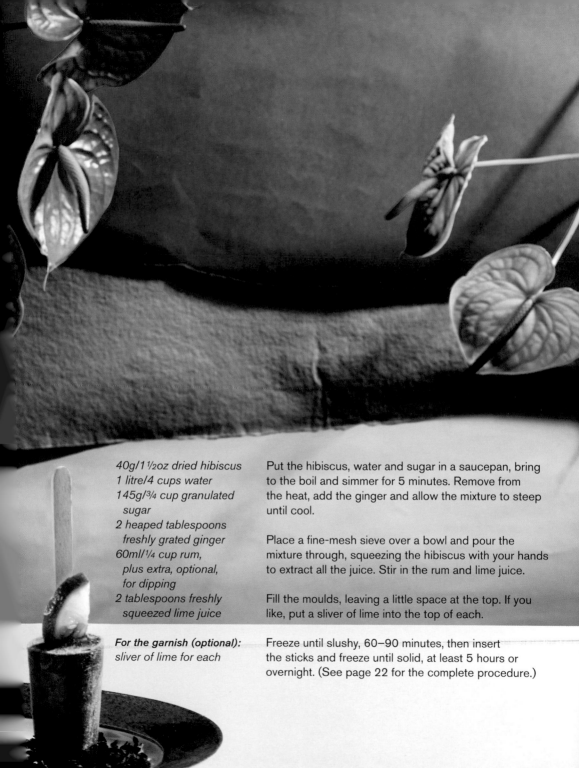

40g/1½oz dried hibiscus
1 litre/4 cups water
145g/¾ cup granulated
  sugar
2 heaped tablespoons
  freshly grated ginger
60ml/¼ cup rum,
  plus extra, optional,
  for dipping
2 tablespoons freshly
  squeezed lime juice

For the garnish (optional):
sliver of lime for each

Put the hibiscus, water and sugar in a saucepan, bring to the boil and simmer for 5 minutes. Remove from the heat, add the ginger and allow the mixture to steep until cool.

Place a fine-mesh sieve over a bowl and pour the mixture through, squeezing the hibiscus with your hands to extract all the juice. Stir in the rum and lime juice.

Fill the moulds, leaving a little space at the top. If you like, put a sliver of lime into the top of each.

Freeze until slushy, 60–90 minutes, then insert the sticks and freeze until solid, at least 5 hours or overnight. (See page 22 for the complete procedure.)

LA PALOMA

Tequila, lime, grapefruit

Makes 8–10

The cocktail La Paloma was named after a popular Mexican folk ballad, meaning "the dove". I wonder why? Perhaps Don Javier, owner of the bar La Capilla in Tequila, Mexico, who is said to have created the cocktail, loved the song. This Margarita alternative adds grapefruit, which creates a refreshing complexity. They go down well at parties – try using leafy sprigs from the garden as the sticks.

120ml/½ cup water
110g/½ cup granulated
  sugar
finely grated zest of
  2 limes
550ml/2¼ cups freshly
  squeezed grapefruit juice
  (from about 3 grapefruits)
120ml/½ cup freshly
  squeezed lime juice
  (from about 4 limes)
90ml/6 tablespoons
  tequila

For the garnish (optional):
sliver of lime and a mint
  leaf for each

Put the water, sugar and lime zest in a small saucepan and gently heat until the sugar has dissolved. Mix together with the grapefruit juice, lime juice and tequila.

Fill the moulds, leaving a little space at the top. If you like, you can put a sliver of lime and a mint leaf into the top of each.

Freeze until slushy, 60–90 minutes, then insert the sticks (or leafy sprigs) and freeze until solid, at least 5 hours or overnight. (See page 22 for the complete procedure.)

TEQUILA SUNRISE

Orange, lime, grenadine, tequila

Makes 8–10

Tequila Sunrise was the drink that famously fuelled the Rolling Stones' legendary 1972 American tour. Truman Capote reported on the tour, and on the drink, so contributing to its vogue. They must have been onto something because its warm ombré hues – the pinks, oranges and yellows – glow from within.

70ml/5 tablespoons water
100g/½ cup granulated sugar
½ teaspoon finely grated lime zest
135ml/½ cup freshly squeezed lime juice (from about 4–5 limes)
450ml/scant 2 cups freshly squeezed orange juice (from about 5–6 oranges)
60ml/¼ cup tequila
1 teaspoon grenadine for each mould

For the garnish (optional):
glacé cherry, and orange, lemon and green apple sliver for each

Put the water, sugar and lime zest in a small saucepan and gently heat until the sugar has dissolved. Mix together with the lime juice, orange juice and tequila.

Pour a teaspoon of grenadine into each mould and then very slowly dribble the orange and lime mixture gently down the inside of the mould, so as not to disturb the grenadine too much, filling the moulds and leaving a little space at the top.

Freeze until slushy, 60–90 minutes, then insert the sticks (try using cocktail sticks or thin wooden skewers so you can have fun layering the garnish before serving) and freeze until solid, at least 5 hours or overnight. (See page 22 for the complete procedure.)

PIÑA COLADA

Pineapple, coconut milk, rum

Makes 8–10

Yes we like Piña Coladas, and getting caught in the rain! Everyone knows the Rupert Holmes song "Escape", and this kitsch poolside cocktail from Puerto Rico makes a perfect poptail escape – you don't have to wait until summer. If you like, serve them on a plate drizzled with rum and roll in shredded sweet coconut.

600g/1lb 5oz fresh pineapple chunks (from about 1 pineapple)
about 110g/½ cup caster or granulated sugar (depending on the sweetness of the pineapple)
350ml/1½ cups unsweetened coconut milk
90ml/6 tablespoons white rum, plus extra, optional, to drizzle
2 tablespoons freshly squeezed lemon juice, or to taste

For the garnish (optional):
glacé cherry, pineapple chunk, paper cocktail umbrella and 1 tablespoon sweet shredded coconut for each

Put all the ingredients in a food processor and blend. Taste and add more sugar or lemon juice if needed – it will depend on the sharpness and sweetness of the pineapple.

Fill the moulds, leaving a little space at the top.

Freeze until slushy, 60–90 minutes, then insert the sticks and freeze until solid, at least 5 hours or overnight. (See page 22 for the complete procedure.)

Serve drizzled in rum, if you like, and/or roll the poptails in sweet shredded coconut, adding optional garnishes to the sticks.

LIMONCELLO DREAMSICLE

Lemon, condensed milk, limoncello

Makes about 10 large or 20 small

As opposed to a spin on a cocktail, this one is totally made up, as its fanciful name implies. These poptails are for those who love anything citrus mixed with cream or milk – easy, mouth-puckering and quite indulgent.

1 x 400-g/14-oz can of sweetened condensed milk
finely grated zest of 2 lemons
150ml/²/₃ cup freshly squeezed lemon juice (from about 3–4 lemons)
350ml/1½ cups water
90ml/6 tablespoons limoncello

For the garnish:
thin slice of lemon for each

Put the condensed milk, lemon zest and juice in a bowl and whisk together by hand until fully combined, then whisk in the water and limoncello until smooth and well blended.

Pour the mixture into the moulds, leaving a little space at the top. Push the lolly sticks though a thin slice of lemon and insert them into the moulds; the lemon slice secures the stick.

Freeze until solid, at least 5 hours or overnight. (See page 22 for the complete procedure.)

BLOOD ORANGE NEGRONI

Blood orange, Campari, gin, vermouth

Makes about 20 small

Blood oranges are precious because they have such a short season, so we like to use miniature moulds and present these poptails as jewels, embedded with a thin sliver of Campari-soaked blood orange and a mint leaf. While they are lovely on their own, you might like to serve them in a little bowl and drizzle a couple of tablespoons of gin over them. They're also lovely dipped into a glass of Prosecco.

600ml/2½ cups freshly squeezed blood orange juice (from about 8 blood oranges)
60ml/¼ cup Campari
2 tablespoons sweet vermouth
2 tablespoons gin
150ml/⅔ cup water
110g/½ cup granulated sugar

For the garnish:
sliver of blood orange and a mint leaf for each

Put the blood orange juice, Campari, sweet vermouth and gin in a bowl or jug. Put the water and sugar in a small saucepan and bring to a simmer for a moment until the sugar has dissolved. Add this syrup to the mix.

Pour the mixture into the moulds, leaving a little space at the top. Drop in a blood orange sliver and a mint leaf.

Freeze until slushy, 60–90 minutes, then insert the sticks and freeze until solid, at least 5 hours or overnight. (See page 22 for the complete procedure.)

PLUM IN THE RUM MOJITO

Plum, mint, rum, lime

Makes 8–10

The ever-popular Mojito of Havana derives its name from the term "mojo".
For Ice Kitchen's first range we were inspired by the traditional version, but
this one is with plums; the undercurrent of mint and rum goes well with
them. Poaching plums intensifies their flavour, and the sweet and sour taste
comes mainly from their skin, which colours this Mojito pink, green or yellow
(depending on the plum). Serve this poptail in a bowl or shot glass with some
extra rum to swizzle it in, which will definitely get your mojo working.

350ml/1½ cups water
150g/¾ cup granulated
  sugar
15g/1 cup mint leaves
330g/11½oz plums,
  stoned
2 tablespoons freshly
  squeezed lime juice
60ml/¼ cup rum, plus
  extra for dipping

For the garnish (optional):
thin sliver of lime and/or
  a mint sprig for each

Put the water and sugar in a saucepan and gently bring
to a simmer. Remove from the heat and plunge in the
mint leaves. Allow to steep for at least 20 minutes, then
strain the mixture through a fine-mesh sieve, pressing
down on the leaves with the back of a spoon or
squeezing them with your hands to extract the juices.

Put the syrup back in the pan and add the plums.
Simmer for 10 minutes, until they break down. Remove
from the heat and allow the mixture to cool for a few
minutes, then transfer to a food processor. Add the
lime juice and rum and blend until smooth.

Pour the mixture into the moulds, leaving a little space
at the top. If you like, drop in a lime sliver and/or
mint sprig.

Freeze until slushy, 60–90 minutes, then insert
the sticks and freeze until solid, at least 5 hours or
overnight. (See page 22 for the complete procedure.)

SEA BREEZE

Grapefruit, cranberry, lime, vodka

Makes 8–10

The Sea Breeze dates back to the 1970s, so put on your platforms and Bee Gees record. This summertime drink may be out of favour now but, frozen into a poptail, it's delightful. If you like, serve them on a shallow plate and drizzle a little vodka over them.

60ml/¼ cup water
100g/½ cup granulated
* sugar*
250ml/1 cup cranberry
* juice (100% and*
* unsweetened)*
150ml/⅔ cup freshly
* squeezed grapefruit juice*
* (from about 1 grapefruit)*
3½ tablespoons freshly
* squeezed lime juice*
* (from about 2 limes)*
3 tablespoons vodka

For the garnish (optional):
sliver of grapefruit or lime

Put the water and sugar in a small saucepan and simmer briefly until the sugar has dissolved. Mix with the cranberry juice, grapefruit juice, lime juice and vodka.

Pour the mixture into the moulds, leaving a little space at the top. If you like, drop in a sliver of grapefruit or lime.

Freeze until slushy, 60–90 minutes, then insert the sticks and freeze until solid, at least 5 hours or overnight. (See page 22 for the complete procedure.)

BLUE LAGOON

Curaçao, lemon, vodka

Makes 8–10

Who can resist drinking or eating anything blue? I was always childishly curious to taste the blue drink, and we had to put this one in for the colour and the fun... With Curaçao – made with the dried aromatic peel of the laraha fruit, which is similar to an orange, and added spices – you're drinking blue, but you're tasting orange. The blue is an artificial colouring. Create your own vacation-land lagoon for dipping the lollies in, decorating it with floating flowers and cocktail mermaids.

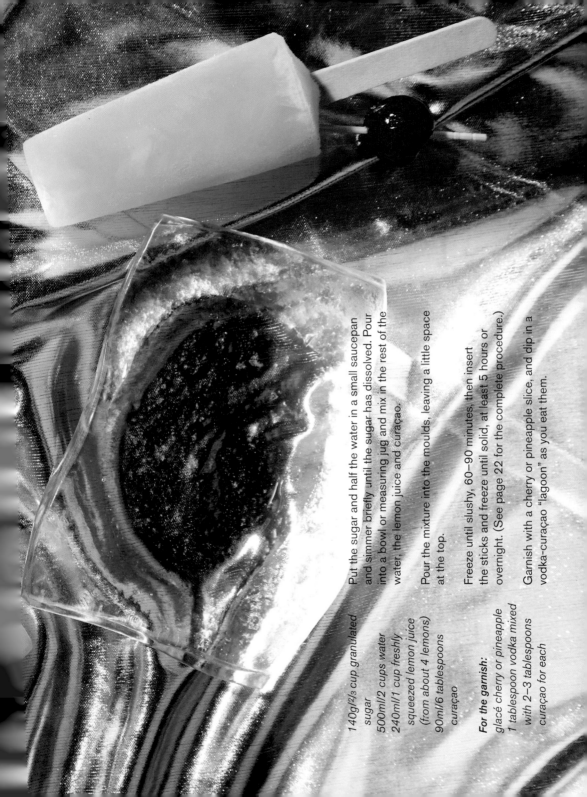

Put the sugar and half the water in a small saucepan and simmer briefly until the sugar has dissolved. Pour into a bowl or measuring jug and mix in the rest of the water, the lemon juice and curaçao.

Pour the mixture into the moulds, leaving a little space at the top.

Freeze until slushy, 60–90 minutes, then insert the sticks and freeze until solid, at least 5 hours or overnight. (See page 22 for the complete procedure.)

Garnish with a cherry or pineapple slice, and dip in a vodka-curaçao "lagoon" as you eat them.

140g/⅔ cup granulated
sugar
500ml/2 cups water
240ml/1 cup freshly
squeezed lemon juice
(from about 4 lemons)
90ml/6 tablespoons
curaçao

For the garnish:
glacé cherry or pineapple
1 tablespoon vodka mixed
with 2–3 tablespoons
curaçao for each

ROASTED BANANA RUMSICLES

Banana, cream, lime, rum

Makes 8–10

You can laugh at the name, but these aren't just for banana lovers. Roasting the bananas intensifies the flavour and creates a melting texture and, of course, roasted bananas cry out for rum.

3 large, ripe bananas
90g/scant ½ cup
  muscovado sugar
175ml/¾ cup whole milk
175ml/¾ cup double
  (heavy) cream
1 tablespoon freshly
  squeezed lime juice
1 teaspoon vanilla extract
90ml/6 tablespoons rum

Preheat your oven to 200°C/400°F/Gas 6. Place the bananas whole on a baking sheet (do not peel them) and roast in the oven for about 20 minutes, until soft and their skins turn black. Remove and allow them to cool, then peel.

Put the banana flesh in a food processor with all the other ingredients and whizz until smooth.

Pour the mixture into the moulds, leaving a little space at the top.

Freeze until slushy, 60–90 minutes, then insert the sticks and freeze until solid, at least 5 hours or overnight. (See page 22 for the complete procedure.)

PINEAPPLE PASTIS

Pineapple, orange, pastis

Makes 8–10

My great friend Alec Chanda, an artist whose culinary talent matches his artistic brilliance, once made me an amazing pineapple and fennel drink. The memory of this union of flavours led to my experimenting with pastis and pineapple. Pastis has the same anise-like flavour as fennel, and the optional tarragon garnish offers an additional anise experience. An original.

*600g/1lb 5oz fresh
  pineapple chunks
  (from about 1 pineapple)
200ml/¾ cup freshly
  squeezed orange
  juice (from about
  2–3 oranges)
4–5 tablespoons caster or
  granulated sugar
90ml/6 tablespoons pastis*

For the garnish (optional):
*7.5-cm/3-inch sprig of
  tarragon for each*

Put the pineapple chunks, orange juice and 4 tablespoons sugar in a food processor and blend to a purée. Taste and add more sugar if needed, depending on the sweetness of the pineapple. Add the pastis and blend again.

Put a sprig of tarragon into each mould, if using, then pour in the pineapple mixture, leaving a little space at the top.

Freeze until slushy, 60–90 minutes, then insert the sticks and freeze until solid, at least 5 hours or overnight. (See page 22 for the complete procedure.)

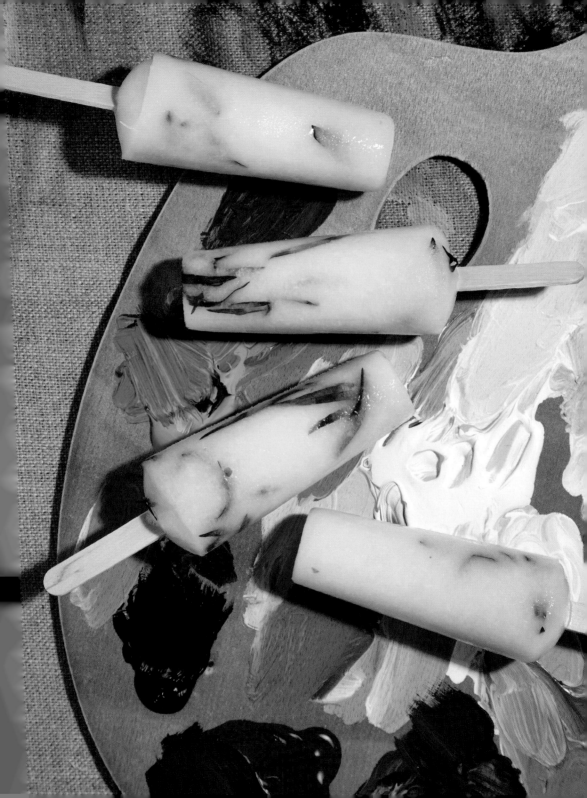

TANGO BRAVO WHISKY

Tangerine, basil, lemon, whisky

Makes 12–15

In this tangerine dream, the basil brings out the sweet and tangy citrus flavours, and is a perfect match for the warm chocolate and vanilla notes from the whisky. Great on its own, but for kicks, dip it in a shot glass of whisky.

160ml/²/₃ cup water
140g/³/₄ cup granulated sugar
1 teaspoon finely grated tangerine zest
15g/¹/₂ packed cup fresh, torn basil leaves
700ml/scant 3 cups freshly squeezed tangerine juice (from about 15 tangerines)
3 tablespoons freshly squeezed lemon juice
3 tablespoons whisky, plus extra for dipping

For the garnish (optional):
sliver of tangerine and a basil leaf for each

Put the water, sugar, tangerine zest and basil leaves in a small saucepan and bring to a simmer. Remove from the heat and allow to cool.

Strain the syrup through a sieve, squeezing the leaves with your fingers to extract all the precious basil juice. Mix the syrup with the tangerine and lemon juices, and the whisky.

Pour the mixture into the moulds, leaving a little space at the top. If you like, drop in a sliver of tangerine and a basil leaf.

Freeze until slushy, 60–90 minutes, then insert the sticks and freeze until solid, at least 5 hours or overnight. (See page 22 for the complete procedure.)

AMARETTO PEACH

Peach, amaretto, almond, cream

Makes 8–10

Years ago, when I moved to New York, amaretto was everywhere; even the coffee beans were flavoured with it. What's old is now new again. This sweet and slightly bitter almond-flavoured amber liqueur from Saronno, in Italy, is made from steeped apricot kernels (and sometimes almonds) and infused with herbs and fruits. It comes in a beautiful rectangular-shaped bottle designed by a craftsman from Murano. For such a powerful flavour, amaretto surprisingly complements the delicate peach.

Although delicious on their own, these poptails are divine served on a small plate drizzled with amaretto and rolled in crunchy crumbled amaretti cookies. You could also try adding the crumbled amaretti to the mixture instead. Be sure to use ripe and fragrant peaches.

500g/1lb 2oz peach flesh, chopped (*from about 4 fragrant peaches*)
60g/5 tablespoons caster or granulated sugar
2 tablespoons freshly squeezed lemon juice
110ml/½ cup amaretto
½ teaspoon almond extract
120ml/½ cup double (*heavy*) cream

To serve:
10 amaretti cookies, finely crumbled with a pestle and mortar or bashed with a rolling pin
2 tablespoons amaretto for each
a drizzle of cream (optional)

Put all the main ingredients in a food processor and blend to a purée.

Pour the mixture into the moulds, leaving a little space at the top.

Freeze until slushy, 60–90 minutes, then insert the sticks and freeze until solid, at least 5 hours or overnight. (See page 22 for the complete procedure.)

To serve, dip in the lollies in the amaretto and roll in the amaretti crumbs. Drizzle with cream, if you like.

LION'S MILK

Arak, yogurt, honey

Makes 8–10

My grandfather Cesar inspired this poptail. He came from Egypt to London, and used to drink arak every night, often accompanied by a yogurt mezze. So I was curious to try the combination as a poptail, and was surprised and delighted with the results. Nicknamed "the milk of lions", arak is an ancient and beloved anise-flavoured drink from the Middle East that turns a milky-white colour when water is added. It is typically made from distilling grapes, although dates, plums and figs are sometimes used, depending on the region. If you have no arak, use pastis, which gives the same results.

500g/2 cups full-fat
  Greek yogurt
150g/½ cup runny honey
  (it tastes great with
  clover honey)
200ml/¾ cup water
90ml/6 tablespoons arak
  or pastis

Put the yogurt in a bowl, add the honey and stir it in with a spoon. Stir in the water, then the arak or pastis, until well blended.

Pour the mixture into the moulds, leaving a little space at the top.

Freeze until slushy, 60–90 minutes, then insert the sticks and freeze until solid, at least 5 hours or overnight. (See page 22 for the complete procedure.)

FIGS GO SOUTH OF THE BORDER

Fig, orange, honey, Cointreau, tequila

Makes 8–10

Figs are amazing in a lolly, as both their flavour and texture are enhanced by freezing, and make a harmonious blend with the orange, honey and Cointreau. It may seem curious dipping these into a shot glass of tequila, but that sets everything off, you'll see. It's *muy bueno*, and too much will drive you *loco*.

110g/4oz figs (use a thin-skinned variety, such as Mission)
240ml/1 cup freshly squeezed orange juice (from about 3 oranges)
3 tablespoons Cointreau (or another orange liqueur)
1½ tablespoons runny honey (clover honey is great)

To serve:
tequila

Wash the figs well, leaving their skins on. Cut off the stems and slice the figs directly into a food processor. Pour in the orange juice, Cointreau and honey and blend together.

Pour the mixture into the moulds, leaving a little space at the top.

Freeze until slushy, 60–90 minutes, then insert the sticks and freeze until solid, at least 5 hours or overnight. (See page 22 for the complete procedure.)

To serve, pour a little tequila into individual shot glasses and dip the pops in as you eat them.

BLACKBERRY BRAMBLE

Blackberries, cassis, gin, lemon

Makes 8–10

The Bramble cocktail was created in the 1980s by the famous London bartender and "Cocktail King", Dick Bradsell. The herby tones within the gin complement the blackberries and lemon, and these are the ideal poptails to make in late summer, when the blackberry season peaks. Leave the seeds in because their crunchy texture adds to the whole "bramble" experience. To "lose yourself in the blackberry patch" and for a delicious experience, I recommend dipping these into a shot glass of gin as you eat them.

400g/14oz blackberries, plus a few extra, optional, to garnish
350ml/1½ cups water
75g/6 tablespoons caster or granulated sugar
3 tablespoons freshly squeezed lemon juice
120ml/½ cup crème de cassis
60ml/¼ cup gin, plus extra, optional, to serve

For the garnish (optional):
sliver of lemon or a bramble leaf for each

Wash the blackberries and put them in a food processor with all the remaining ingredients. Whizz to a purée.

Pour the mixture into the moulds, leaving a little space at the top. If you like, drop in a sliver of lemon or a bramble leaf.

Freeze until slushy, 60–90 minutes, then insert the sticks and freeze until solid, at least 5 hours or overnight. (See page 22 for the complete procedure.)

If you like, garnish with a fresh blackberry and serve dipped into a shot of gin.

APRICOT CHAMOMILE MUSCAT

Apricot, chamomile, Muscat de Beaumes de Venise

Makes 8–10

Muscat de Beaumes de Venise is made with the sweet muscat grapes that grow above the sunny limestone slabs in the southern half of the Rhône valley. Apricots, chamomile and muscat grapes grow together and make a natural union; they represent all things fragrant, good and romantic. These poptails are charming on their own, or served along with a glass of Muscat de Beaumes de Venise or, better still if you have some, dipped in a little glass of St. Germain (the French elderflower liqueur).

240ml/1 cup water
½ cup fresh or dried chamomile flowers, or 4 chamomile tea bags
100g/½ cup granulated sugar
460g/1lb apricots, stoned and quartered
240ml/1 cup Muscat de Beaumes de Venise

For the garnish (optional):
a freshly picked leaf for each

Put the water and chamomile flowers or tea bags in a saucepan and simmer for 5 minutes. Remove from the heat and allow to cool.

Pour the infusion through a fine-mesh sieve, pressing on the chamomile to extract the juice, and return the infusion to the pan (or if using tea bags, simply pull them out and squeeze them to extract the juice). Stir in the sugar and apricots and cook over a low heat for 5–10 minutes until the apricots are soft. Stir in the Muscat, remove from the heat and set aside to cool. Blend the cooled mixture in a food processor.

Pour the mixture into the moulds, leaving a little space at the top. If you like, drop a leaf in.

Freeze until slushy, 60–90 minutes, then insert the sticks and freeze until solid, at least 5 hours or overnight. (See page 22 for the complete procedure.)

MIXED BERRIES IN RIESLING

Berries, lemon, Riesling

Makes 8–10

The mélange of the berry flavours draws out the fruity notes from the Riesling wine. Bursting with flavour, this summery poptail can also be enjoyed during the cold winter months, since frozen berries work very well too. These look especially beautiful served on a bed of crushed ice, sprinkled with berries, flowers or mint leaves.

450g/1lb mixed berries, such as blueberries, redcurrants, raspberries, blackberries or strawberries
90g/½ cup caster or granulated sugar
1½ tablespoons freshly squeezed lemon juice
290ml/1¼ cups Riesling wine

For the garnish (optional):
sliver of lemon and a mint leaf for each

If you are including strawberries, cut them into quarters. Put all the berries in a bowl, sprinkle over the sugar, then the lemon juice and 120ml/½ cup of the Riesling. Leave to macerate for a few hours, until the berries are soft and the flavours have mingled. Now stir in the remaining Riesling.

Pour the mixture into the moulds, making sure you distribute the berries evenly, leaving a little space at the top. If you like, drop in a sliver of lemon and a mint leaf.

Freeze until slushy, 60–90 minutes, then insert the sticks and freeze until solid, at least 5 hours or overnight. (See page 22 for the complete procedure.)

ROSÉ WITH STRAWBERRIES & BASIL

Rosé wine, strawberries, basil

Makes 8–10

Rosé wine is so *au courant* now, and the subtle, warm and sweet undercurrent of basil brings out and complements both the strawberry and rosé flavours. Serve as they are or dipped in a glass of rosé wine. A stylish treat to bring in the summer.

400g/14oz strawberries, hulled and quartered (or eighths if large)
60g/5 tablespoons granulated sugar
120ml/½ cup water
15g/1 loosely packed cup basil leaves
2 tablespoons freshly squeezed lemon juice
240ml/1 cup rosé wine

For the garnish (optional):
basil leaf for each

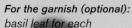

Put the strawberries in a bowl, sprinkle over half the sugar and set aside.

Meanwhile, put the remaining sugar, water and basil leaves in a small saucepan and bring to a brief simmer, then remove from the heat and allow to cool; the longer the syrup stands, the more the basil will flavour it.

Place a sieve over the bowl of strawberries and pour the syrup through. Squeeze the leaves with your fingers to extract all the basil juice. Stir in the lemon juice and rosé wine and set aside for at least 30 minutes, to allow the flavours to develop together.

Divide the mixture equally between the moulds, leaving a little space at the top. If you like, drop a small basil leaf into the top of each.

Freeze until slushy, 60–90 minutes, then insert the sticks and freeze until solid, at least 5 hours or overnight. (See page 22 for the complete procedure.)

APEROL ORANGE TARRAGON SPRITZ

Aperol, orange, lemon, tarragon

Makes 8–10

This is like eating pure Mediterranean sunshine. Aperol, the orange-red aperitif that originated in Padua, Italy in 1919, is made with bitter oranges, rhubarb, the cinchona plant and various secret ingredients. This poptail is perfect on its own, but for the "spritz" experience, pour yourself a glass of Prosecco and dip this lolly into it as you lick. The tarragon garnish contrasts with and highlights the orange flavours.

120ml/½ cup water
60g/5 tablespoons granulated sugar
1 teaspoon finely grated orange zest
600ml/2½ cups freshly squeezed orange juice (from about 6–7 oranges)
3–4 tablespoons freshly squeezed lemon juice (from about 1–2 lemons)
135ml/½ cup Aperol

For the garnish:
7.5-cm/3-inch sprig of tarragon for each

Put the water, sugar and orange zest in a saucepan and briefly simmer until the sugar dissolves, then remove from the heat and allow to cool.

Stir the cooled syrup into the orange juice, lemon juice and Aperol.

Place a tarragon sprig in each mould and pour the mixture in, leaving a little space at the top.

Freeze until slushy, 60–90 minutes, then insert the sticks and freeze until solid, at least 5 hours or overnight. (See page 22 for the complete procedure.)

ROYAL RED CRANBERRY SPRITZ

Cranberries, orange, Champagne

Makes 8–10

As part of a holiday meal, this festive and visually regal poptail is perfect for Christmas, New Year, or just when it's snowing. It could be served between courses as a palate cleanser, or as a refreshing end to a feast. Present it in a glass of Champagne.

200g/2 cups cranberries (fresh or frozen)
100g/½ cup granulated sugar
1 teaspoon finely grated orange zest
560ml/2⅓ cups freshly squeezed orange juice (from about 6–7 oranges)
3 tablespoons orange liqueur or apricot brandy
Champagne, to serve

For the garnish (optional):
couple of cranberries, a mint leaf or sliver of grapefruit for each

Put the cranberries, sugar, orange zest and juice in a saucepan and simmer for 10–15 minutes, until the cranberries have burst and their juices are released. Remove from the heat and allow to cool down to room temperature.

Blend the mixture to a purée in a food processor, then strain through a fine-mesh sieve, stirring and pressing with the back of a spoon to extract all the juices. Stir in the orange liqueur or apricot brandy.

Pour the mixture into the moulds, leaving a little space at the top. If you like, drop a couple of cranberries, a mint leaf or a sliver of grapefruit into the top of each.

Freeze until slushy, 60–90 minutes, then insert the sticks and freeze until solid, at least 5 hours or overnight. (See page 22 for the complete procedure.)

NAPOLEON'S RETREAT

Strawberries, Champagne, cream

Makes 8–10

This delicate blend was invented by Napoleon's chief steward and taste-maker, the Marquis de Cussy, at the time when Champagne was drunk in secret by nobles who were afraid of the guillotine. It became Napoleon's favourite dessert cocktail, and we've frozen it into a poptail. Enjoy the pops on their own or pour out glasses of Champagne, Prosecco or white wine, and swirl them as you get ready to "retreat" into bliss.

450g/1lb strawberries, hulled and chopped
100g/½ cup caster or granulated sugar, plus 3 tablespoons
200ml/¾ cup Champagne or white wine
120ml/½ cup double (heavy) cream

Put the strawberries in a bowl, sprinkle them with the 100g/½ cup sugar and stir, then pour in the Champagne or white wine. Allow the mixture to sit for 30 minutes so that the flavours develop, then blend to a purée in a food processor.

Stir the 3 tablespoons sugar into the cream.

Pour the strawberry mixture into the moulds, leaving enough space to drizzle a little cream on top of each.

Freeze until slushy, 60–90 minutes, then insert the sticks and freeze until solid, at least 5 hours or overnight. (See page 22 for the complete procedure.)

ORANGE & BLOSSOM MIMOSA

Orange, lemon, orange blossom water, Champagne

Makes 8–10

The Mimosa cocktail is thought to have been invented in 1925, by a bartender at the Hôtel Ritz in Paris – the mysterious Frank Meier – who probably named it after the cadmium-yellow mimosa flower. In our version, the orange blossom flavour shines through so that you can imagine you're walking through an orange grove. These are wonderful on their own, or swizzled into a glass of Champagne or sparkling wine.

110g/½ cup granulated sugar
1 teaspoon finely grated orange zest
75ml/5 tablespoons water
500ml/2 cups freshly squeezed orange juice (from about 6 oranges)
3 tablespoons freshly squeezed lemon juice
1 tablespoon orange blossom water
300ml/1¼ cups Champagne or sparkling wine

For the garnish (optional):
thin sliver of orange or a flower blossom for each

Put the sugar, orange zest and water in a small saucepan and briefly simmer until the sugar has dissolved. Stir the syrup into the orange and lemon juices, then stir in the orange blossom water and the Champagne or sparkling wine.

Pour the mixture into the moulds, leaving a little space at the top. If you like, drop in a sliver of orange or a flower blossom.

Freeze until slushy, 60–90 minutes, then insert the sticks and freeze until solid, at least 5 hours or overnight. (See page 22 for the complete procedure.)

POMMES-POMMES

Apple, vanilla, Calvados, Champagne

Makes 8–10

Inspired by the most popular drink at the Bar Hemingway at the Hôtel Ritz in Paris, bartender Colin Field invented a concoction of Champagne, Calvados, fresh apple juice, sugar and loads of mint. He called it "The Serendipity" and said it was "France-in-a-glass". We've exchanged vanilla for the mint and called it the "Pommes-Pommes" after an older version of the cocktail.

A good way to serve this is in a Champagne flute with 2 tablespoons of Calvados, and a big splash of ice-cold Champagne or other sparkling white wine. Twirl the lollies in the glass as you dream of springtime in Paris. If you like, place a rose by the side of the glass as they do at the Ritz.

2 tart apples (such as Granny Smith), peeled, cored and chopped
65g/⅓ cup granulated sugar
350ml/1½ cups pressed apple juice
1 teaspoon vanilla extract
3 tablespoons Calvados, plus extra, optional, to serve
Champagne, optional, to serve

For the garnish (optional):
thin apple sliver for each

Put the chopped apples in a small saucepan with the sugar and 120ml/½ cup of the apple juice and simmer over a low heat until the apples are soft, about 10 minutes.

Remove from the heat and allow the mixture to cool, then blend in a food processor together with the remaining apple juice, vanilla and Calvados.

Pour the mixture into the moulds, leaving a little space at the top. If you like, drop a sliver of apple into the top of each.

Freeze until slushy, 60–90 minutes, then insert the sticks and freeze until solid, at least 5 hours or overnight. (See page 22 for the complete procedure.) Serve dipped in a glass of Calvados and Champagne, if you like.

PEACH BELLINI

Peach, lemon, Prosecco

Makes 8–10

It was around 1940 at Harry's Bar in Venice that the Bellini was invented, named for its colour after the painter Bellini's flesh tones. There are some who say that a peach is the fruit that most resembles a lady's bottom or bosom, with its delicate flesh, shape and perfume. For the full Bellini, dip these into a glass of Prosecco.

600g/1lb 5oz sweet, fragrant peach flesh, chopped (skin on, from about 4 peaches)
110g/½ cup granulated sugar
60ml/¼ cup freshly squeezed lemon juice (from about 1–2 lemons)
250ml/1 cup Prosecco or white wine

For the garnish:
twist of pared lemon zest for each

Put the chopped peaches in a bowl with the sugar and lemon juice. Set aside for about 20 minutes to macerate.

Transfer the mixture to a food processor, add the Prosecco or white wine and blend until smooth. Pour the mixture into the moulds, leaving a little space at the top. If you like, drop a twist of lemon zest on top.

Freeze until slushy, 60–90 minutes, then insert the sticks and freeze until solid, at least 5 hours or overnight. (See page 22 for the complete procedure.)

PIMM'S ON A STICK

Pimm's, mint, apple, orange, strawberries, cucumber, lemon

Makes 8–10

You don't have to be an English "Hooray Henry" to enjoy this poptail; Pimm's is still going strong after nearly 200 years. The chopped garnishes mingled with the lemonade and submerged in Pimm's are a true expression of an English summer garden party. Re-dip into Pimm's as you go.

250ml/1 cup water
100g/½ cup granulated sugar
15g/1 cup torn mint leaves
150g/5½oz sliced strawberries
60g/2oz thinly sliced apple
60g/2oz orange, peeled and thinly sliced
60g/2oz thinly sliced cucumber
60ml/¼ cup freshly squeezed lemon juice (from about 1–2 lemons)
120ml/½ cup Pimm's

For the garnish (optional):
mint leaf for each

Put the water and half the sugar in a small saucepan and bring to the boil. Take off the heat, drop in the mint leaves and steep for an hour, or longer.

Meanwhile, put the strawberries, and apple, orange and cucumber slices in a bowl and stir in the rest of the sugar, the lemon juice and Pimm's. Leave to macerate for 30 minutes or more.

Strain the syrup into the fruit and Pimm's mixture, squeezing the mint leaves with your hands to extract their juices.

Pour the mixture into the moulds, making sure you divide the fruit pieces evenly and leaving a little space at the top. If you like, drop in a mint leaf.

Freeze until slushy, 60–90 minutes, then insert the sticks and freeze until solid, at least 5 hours or overnight. (See page 22 for the complete procedure.)

FLOWER GARDEN

Champagne, orange blossom water, flowers

Makes 8–10

These poptails will add a little magic to an elegant occasion, like a wedding party. You can use any type of edible flower, such as pansy, nasturtium, violet, rose, chamomile, chrysanthemum or marigold – flowers all so beautiful and fragrant. Seeing them captured in transparent ice is reminiscent of beauty immortalized.

480ml/2 cups water
120g/²/₃ cup granulated
  sugar
240ml/1 cup Champagne
  (flat Champagne works
  best)
1 tablespoon freshly
  squeezed lemon juice
½ teaspoon orange
  blossom or rose water
handful of edible flowers
  or petals

Put the water and sugar in a small saucepan and simmer until the sugar has dissolved. Take off the heat and allow the syrup to cool, then mix the syrup into the Champagne and stir in the lemon juice and orange blossom or rose water.

Sprinkle the flowers and petals into the lolly moulds and pour the Champagne mixture over them, leaving a little space at the top.

Freeze until slushy, 60–90 minutes, then insert the sticks and freeze until solid, at least 5 hours or overnight. (See page 22 for the complete procedure.)

THE EXISTENTIALIST

Ruby grapefruit, pastis

Makes 6–8

The idea for this came up while I was staying with artist friends Thierry and Carmen in Payrac, sitting on their terrace and sipping pastis. This poptail is curiously addictive, like absinthe. I've called it The Existentialist as its flavour is "abstract" and gives you something to ponder as you suck. Its character is so individual that it requires no further "dipping". The grapefruit, which is an excellent fruit for a poptail because of its complexity, and the pastis, which gives it potency, meet in an unusual combination that is a personal favourite.

60ml/¼ cup water
65g/⅓ cup granulated
  sugar
360ml/1½ cups
  freshly squeezed ruby
  grapefruit juice (from
  about 2–3 grapefruits)
3 tablespoons pastis

For the garnish (optional):
strip of grapefruit zest for
  each

Put the water and sugar in a small saucepan and briefly simmer until the sugar has dissolved. Take off the heat and allow the syrup to cool, then mix with the grapefruit juice and pastis.

Pour the mixture into the moulds, leaving a little space at the top.

Freeze until slushy, 60–90 minutes, then insert the sticks and freeze until solid, at least 5 hours or overnight. (See page 22 for the complete procedure.)

LYCHEE MARTINI

Lychees, lime, vodka, rose water

Makes about 10 large or 25 small

The suave Martini is made exotic here. The delicately perfumed lychee, with the lime, makes this martini-on-a-stick subtle, light and refreshing, and the rose water gives it a feminine charm. Perfect for lazing on a sunny afternoon or, for a hedonistic evening, twizzle the pops in vodka.

2 x 567-g cans lychees, drained/4 cups drained canned lychees, plus 360ml/1 ½ cups of the lychee syrup
1 teaspoon finely grated lime zest
90ml/6 tablespoons freshly squeezed lime juice (from about 2–3 limes)
1–2 tablespoons sugar (if needed)
90ml/6 tablespoons vodka
2 teaspoons rose water (not rose extract)

For the garnish (optional):
sliver of lime or a rose petal for each

Put the drained lychees, lychee syrup, lime zest and juice in a food processor and blend to a smooth purée.

Strain the purée into a bowl through a sieve, stirring it through with a spoon, and pushing down on the solids to extract as much juice as possible from the pulp. Taste the mixture; you may want to add a tablespoon or two of sugar, depending on how sweet the lychee syrup is. Stir the vodka and rose water into the mixture.

Pour the mixture into the moulds, leaving a little space at the top. If you like, drop in a sliver of lime or a delicate rose petal.

Freeze until slushy, 60–90 minutes, then insert the sticks and freeze until solid, at least 5 hours or overnight. (See page 22 for the complete procedure.)

LITTLE MINT JULEPS

Mint, lemon, Bourbon

Makes about 20 small

Mint Julep is the traditional drink of the American South, and the cocktail of the Kentucky Derby. These refreshing pops are best served small and dipped into a nice Bourbon. You can serve the Bourbon in a silver cup, as they do for the Derby.

94

480ml/2 cups water
100g/½ cup granulated
  sugar
30g/1½ packed cups
  fresh mint leaves
2 tablespoons freshly
  squeezed lemon juice
60ml/¼ cup Bourbon
  whiskey

For the garnish (optional):
few chopped mint leaves
  for each

Put the water and sugar in a small saucepan and simmer briefly until the sugar has dissolved. Stir the mint leaves into the syrup, remove from the heat and set aside to cool.

Strain the syrup through a sieve into a bowl, squeezing the mint leaves to extract all their juices, then stir in the lemon juice and Bourbon.

Pour the mixture into the moulds, leaving a little space at the top. If you like, sprinkle in some chopped mint.

Freeze until slushy, 60–90 minutes, then insert the sticks and freeze until solid, at least 5 hours or overnight. (See page 22 for the complete procedure.)

MANGO MARGARITA

Mango, lime, tequila, triple sec

Makes 8–10

The mango originated in East Asia, particularly in India where it was the inspiration for the Paisley pattern, and is adored in all the countries where it grows. It's important to find a good-quality mango, such as the Alphonso variety. Its marriage to the Margarita is the perfect union for a frozen fiesta. Squeeze extra lime over them before serving and, to get happy, dip them in tequila – but don't end up on the floor.

350ml/1½ cups water
65g/⅓ cup granulated sugar, or more, depending on the sweetness of the mango
1 teaspoon finely grated lime zest
400g/2¼ cups chopped mango flesh (from about 2 mangos)
60ml/¼ cup freshly squeezed lime juice (from about 2 limes)
90ml/6 tablespoons tequila, plus extra to serve
2 tablespoons triple sec
lime wedges, to serve

For the garnish (optional):
sliver of lime and sprinkling of chilli (chili) powder for each

Put 60ml/¼ cup of the water in a small saucepan with the sugar and lime zest and simmer until the sugar has dissolved. Take off the heat and allow the syrup to cool.

Put the mango, lime juice, tequila, triple sec, cooled syrup and remaining water in a food processor and blend until smooth.

Pour the mixture into the moulds, leaving a little space at the top. If you like, drop in a sliver of lime and add a sprinkling of chilli powder.

Freeze until slushy, 60–90 minutes, then insert the sticks and freeze until solid, at least 5 hours or overnight. (See page 22 for the complete procedure.)

Serve with the lime wedges for squeezing, and tequila for dipping them in.

CHOCOLATE CHILLI WHISKY SWIZZLES

Whisky, chocolate, chilli, bacon

Makes about 10 large or 20 small

Stopping short of smoke coming out of our ears, we've created a blend where the chilli matches the whisky in oomph. Use a good-quality whisky, as its flavour will be emphasized when partnered with the chocolate. These are lovely on their own, but swizzling them into a shot of whisky and then into crumbled crispy bacon (or with a piece of bacon) validates the expression "too much is never enough".

500ml/2 cups whole milk
250ml/1 cup double (heavy) cream
45g/¼ cup caster or granulated sugar
6–8 generous pinches of cayenne pepper
150g/5¼oz good-quality dark chocolate, finely chopped
75ml/5 tablespoons whisky, plus extra, optional, to serve

For the garnish:
jalapeño chilli (chile) and piece of crispy bacon for each

Put the milk and cream in a saucepan and bring to a simmer. Remove from the heat, add the sugar, cayenne pepper and chopped chocolate and stir for a couple of minutes until well blended and creamy. Set the mixture aside to cool; the longer it sits, the smoother and creamier your poptail will be. Stir in the whisky.

Pour the mixture into the moulds, leaving a little space at the top.

Freeze until slushy, 60–90 minutes, then insert the sticks and freeze until solid, at least 5 hours or overnight. (See page 22 for the complete procedure.)

Serve with a chilli and piece of bacon, or dipped into whisky then crumbled bacon.

CHOCOLATE NEGRONI

Chocolate, Campari, sweet vermouth, gin

Makes about 10 large or 20 small

This one is for real men, those who like their chocolate dark, sophisticated and bittersweet. All three Negroni spirits boldly express themselves, and the sliver of tangy orange garnish helps sweeten it up. These are great on their own and even more delicious if you dip them into a shot glass of sweet vermouth as you eat them.

500ml/2 cups whole milk
250ml/1 cup double
   (heavy) cream
1 teaspoon finely grated
   orange zest
150g/5¼oz good-quality
   dark chocolate, finely
   chopped
1 teaspoon vanilla extract
50g/¼ cup granulated
   sugar
60ml/¼ cup Campari
60ml/¼ cup sweet
   vermouth
60ml/¼ cup gin

For the garnish:
sliver of orange for each

Put the milk, cream and orange zest in a saucepan and bring to a simmer. Remove from the heat, add the chocolate, vanilla and sugar and stir until blended and creamy. Set aside to cool, then chill in the fridge. The longer the mixture sits, the smoother it becomes. Stir in the Campari, sweet vermouth and gin until blended.

Pour the mixture into the moulds, leaving a little space at the top. Insert a sliver of orange into each.

Freeze until slushy, 60–90 minutes, then insert the sticks and freeze until solid, at least 5 hours or overnight. (See page 22 for the complete procedure.)

BOURBON VANILLA

Cream, vanilla, Bourbon

Makes 8–10

Bourbon is a corn-based whiskey that has a great affinity with the creamy flavour of vanilla, but we tend to use Glenfiddich Scotch whisky instead, because it works beautifully and there is an abundance of it in our family – my mother Claudia has won many Glenfiddich cookbook awards, usually accompanied by bottles of this fine product. I suggest rolling these in crumbled cookies, such as amaretti, cantucci or vanilla wafers, for a lovely crunchy contrast to the creaminess.

400ml/1¾ cups whole milk
2 tablespoons cornflour (cornstarch)
300ml/1¼ cups double (heavy) cream
120g/⅔ cup granulated sugar
60ml/¼ cup Bourbon whiskey or whisky
2 teaspoons vanilla extract

For dipping (optional):
5–10 amaretti, cantucci or vanilla cookies, crumbled

Put 3 tablespoons of the milk in a small bowl and mix in the cornflour (cornstarch) to form a smooth paste. Put the remaining milk, cream and sugar in a small saucepan and heat until just about to simmer, then stir in the cornflour paste. Stir constantly as the mixture gently bubbles, until the milk and cream have thickened, about 2 minutes.

Take off the heat and pour the mixture into a bowl. Stir in the Bourbon or whisky and the vanilla extract. Allow to cool.

Pour the cooled mixture into the moulds, leaving a little space at the top.

Freeze until slushy, 60–90 minutes, then insert the sticks and freeze until solid, at least 5 hours or overnight. (See page 22 for the complete procedure.)

Serve dipped in the crushed cookies, if you like.

RUM RAISIN

Raisins, rum, cream, egg yolks

Makes 8–10

This traditional combination has its deep roots in Sicily, where they use the delicious sweet Malaga raisins. What makes this poptail so lovely is that the rum-soaked raisins, which gather towards the end, burst with alcohol as you eat them and add contrast to the milky rum custard. If you have time, soak them overnight. Enjoy these poptails on their own or serve on a plate with extra rum-soaked raisins.

40g/¼ cup raisins
75ml/5 tablespoons rum
300ml/1¼ cups whole milk
300ml/1¼ cups double (heavy) cream
120g/½ cup granulated sugar
5 egg yolks
1 teaspoon vanilla extract

Put the raisins and rum in a small bowl and leave to soak for at least 3 hours or overnight if possible; the longer the better.

Put the milk, cream and sugar in a small saucepan and heat until almost boiling. Remove from the heat.

In a medium bowl, briefly whisk the egg yolks, then add a ladleful of the hot milk mixture, whisking constantly. Pour this back into the pan and heat again over a low heat, stirring constantly, until it has thickened enough to easily coat the back of a spoon (a thermometer should read about 76°C/170°F). Do not let it boil or the eggs will scramble.

Pour the custard immediately into a bowl, stir in the vanilla and allow it to cool and thicken in the fridge for at least 2 hours or overnight.

Add the raisin and rum mixture to the cold custard and stir gently. Spoon the mixture into the moulds, making sure you divide the raisins evenly and leaving a little space at the top.

Freeze until slushy, 60–90 minutes, then insert the sticks and freeze until solid, at least 5 hours or overnight. (See page 22 for the complete procedure.)

ORANGE LIQUEUR CREAMSICLES

Orange, sour cream, Cointreau

Makes 8–10

The nostalgic lolly of every childhood for generations, the creamsicle adapts easily to alcohol and chocolate. In our version, the sour cream creates a light texture. For extra indulgence, try dipping these into molten white chocolate infused with orange liqueur. Would it then be too decadent to dip these into candied orange peel while the chocolate's still molten?

*115g/½–⅔ cup
  granulated sugar
2 teaspoons finely grated
  orange zest
300g/10½oz sour cream
350ml/1½ cups freshly
  squeezed orange juice
  (from about 4 oranges)
75ml/5 tablespoons
  Cointreau or other
  orange liqueur*

*For the garnish (optional):
sliver of orange for each*

*For dipping:
white chocolate, melted
  with a little Cointreau or
  other orange liqueur
4 heaped tablespoons
  chopped candied orange
  peel (optional)*

Put the sugar and orange zest in a food processor and blend until the sugar turns light orange, and the orange oil is released. Add the sour cream and blend for a few seconds. Add the orange juice and Cointreau or orange liqueur and blend again until fully combined.

Pour the mixture into the moulds, leaving a little space at the top. If you like, drop in a sliver of orange.

Freeze until slushy, 60–90 minutes, then insert the sticks and freeze until solid, at least 5 hours or overnight. (See page 22 for the complete procedure.)

Serve dipped in the melted white chocolate and liqueur mixture and then, if you like, into the candied peel.

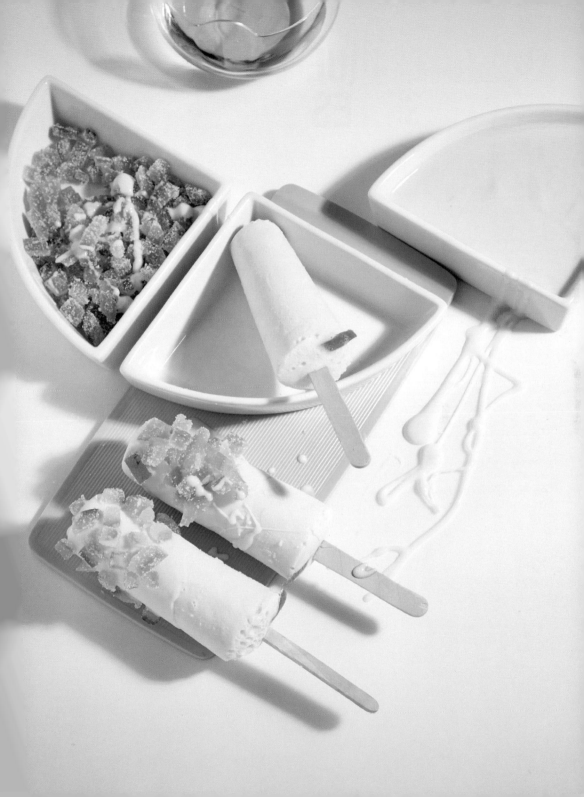

GRAND MARNIER CUSTARD & RASPBERRIES

Cream custard, Grand Marnier, raspberries, limoncello

Makes 8–10

A very indulgent silky-smooth poptail that evolved from a recipe we created for the tearoom at Claridge's Hotel. We were very proud because when the head chef tasted a sample, we thought he actually had tears in his eyes as he complimented us on the clarity of the flavours. We felt as if we had just won a celebrity chef TV programme, and walked on air all the way home.

250g/9oz raspberries
3 tablespoons limoncello (vodka can be substituted)
400ml/1¾ cups whole milk
1½ tablespoons cornflour (cornstarch)
200ml/¾ cup double (heavy) cream
100g/½ cup granulated sugar
3 egg yolks
1 teaspoon vanilla extract
2½ tablespoons Grand Marnier

Put the raspberries in a small bowl with the limoncello and leave to macerate while you make the custard.

Put 3 tablespoons of the milk in a small bowl and mix in the cornflour (cornstarch) to form a smooth paste.

Put the remaining milk, cream and sugar in a small saucepan and heat until just about to simmer, then stir in the cornflour paste. Stir constantly as the mixture gently bubbles, until the milk and cream have thickened, about 2 minutes.

In a medium bowl, briefly whisk the egg yolks, then add a ladleful of the hot milk, whisking constantly. Pour this back into the pan and heat again over a low heat, stirring constantly, until it has thickened and turned into a silky-smooth custard; do not let it boil. Take off the heat, stir in the vanilla and Grand Marnier and allow the custard to cool in the fridge.

Spoon the cooled custard into the moulds, dropping in some raspberries and their juice in between each spoonful so they are evenly distributed, and leaving a little space at the top.

Freeze until slushy, 60–90 minutes, then insert the sticks and freeze until solid, at least 5 hours or overnight. (See page 22 for the complete procedure.)

KAHLÚA COFFEE POPS

Coffee, cream, Kahlúa

Makes 8–10

Kahlúa, the coffee-flavoured liqueur from Mexico, became especially popular in the 1940s and was used to make cocktails like Black Russian, Mudslide, White Russian and Dirty Mother. Our simple but divine Kahlúa coffee pops are made with instant coffee because it gives an intense flavour boost. They are delightful as they are, but for an unforgettable experience dip them into an espresso cup or shot glass with a splash of Kahlúa. They're so easy to make. Serve them at the end of a meal – everyone loves them!

250ml/1 cup whole milk
2 tablespoons granulated
  sugar
3 tablespoons best-quality
  strong instant coffee
250ml/1 cup double
  (heavy) cream
60ml/¼ cup Kahlúa

Put the milk and sugar in a small saucepan and bring to a simmer. Take off the heat and stir in the instant coffee until it is fully dissolved. Mix in the cream and Kahlúa.

Pour the mixture into the moulds, leaving a little space at the top.

Freeze until slushy, 60–90 minutes, then insert the sticks and freeze until solid, at least 5 hours or overnight. (See page 22 for the complete procedure.)

IRISH COFFEE

Coffee, cream, whiskey

Makes 8–10

Irish coffee was conceived in the 1940s, when chef Joe Sheridan – who worked at the airport in County Limerick – welcomed a group of shivering Americans who had just disembarked from a Pan Am flying boat during a dismal winter evening. They wanted to warm up, and the rest is history. The blend of dark rich coffee, Irish whiskey, a little brown sugar and the all-important stripe of cream that stays on the top, is perfect frozen on a stick, accompanied by shortbread cookies or Irish ginger snaps. Dip them into extra whiskey as you go.

70g/½ cup brown sugar
500ml/2 cups freshly brewed extra strong espresso coffee
60ml/¼ cup whiskey, preferably Irish
120ml/½ cup double (heavy) cream

Add the brown sugar to the freshly brewed coffee, stir until the sugar has dissolved, then stir in the whiskey.

Put the cream in a small bowl and beat with a fork until slightly thickened.

Pour the coffee mixture into the moulds, leaving some room on top for the cream. Spoon the cream in very slowly against the side of each mould; it will float back to the top.

Freeze until slushy, 60–90 minutes, then insert the sticks and freeze until solid, at least 5 hours or overnight. (See page 22 for the complete procedure.)

EGGNOG

Cream, egg yolks, nutmeg, rum, Grand Marnier

Makes about 10 large or 15 small

These festive poptails are ideal to celebrate the Christmas season. Eggnog
descends from medieval times, and almost every Western country has its own
version of it, using different alcohols such as whisky, Bourbon, rum, brandy,
cognac, sherry or white wine, and an array of different spices. In ours, nutmeg
is the special characteristic of this holiday delight. We recommend that you
smash up some holiday cookies in a mortar and pestle and then roll the
poptails in the crumbs before serving.

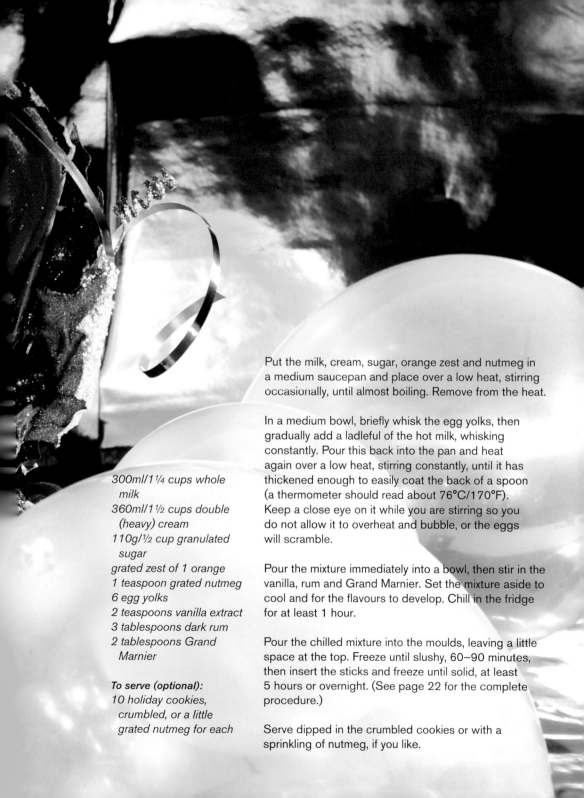

300ml/1¼ cups whole
   milk
360ml/1½ cups double
   (heavy) cream
110g/½ cup granulated
   sugar
grated zest of 1 orange
1 teaspoon grated nutmeg
6 egg yolks
2 teaspoons vanilla extract
3 tablespoons dark rum
2 tablespoons Grand
   Marnier

To serve (optional):
10 holiday cookies,
   crumbled, or a little
   grated nutmeg for each

Put the milk, cream, sugar, orange zest and nutmeg in a medium saucepan and place over a low heat, stirring occasionally, until almost boiling. Remove from the heat.

In a medium bowl, briefly whisk the egg yolks, then gradually add a ladleful of the hot milk, whisking constantly. Pour this back into the pan and heat again over a low heat, stirring constantly, until it has thickened enough to easily coat the back of a spoon (a thermometer should read about 76°C/170°F). Keep a close eye on it while you are stirring so you do not allow it to overheat and bubble, or the eggs will scramble.

Pour the mixture immediately into a bowl, then stir in the vanilla, rum and Grand Marnier. Set the mixture aside to cool and for the flavours to develop. Chill in the fridge for at least 1 hour.

Pour the chilled mixture into the moulds, leaving a little space at the top. Freeze until slushy, 60–90 minutes, then insert the sticks and freeze until solid, at least 5 hours or overnight. (See page 22 for the complete procedure.)

Serve dipped in the crumbled cookies or with a sprinkling of nutmeg, if you like.

ZABAGLIONE

Egg yolks, cream, Marsala

Makes 8–10

When I was a toddler, my mother Claudia made me zabaglione every afternoon as a way to sneak healthy egg yolks into my diet. Marsala, from which the zabaglione gets its special flavour, is the delicious dark, thick and aged dessert wine from southern Sicily. I have such fond memories of this taste and it's a personal favourite as a poptail. Please try it! You can surround it with fresh berries if you like.

180ml/¾ cup Marsala
100g/½ cup granulated sugar
4 egg yolks
120ml/½ cup whole milk
240ml/1 cup double (heavy) cream

In a medium saucepan, whisk together the Marsala, sugar, egg yolks and milk. Place over a low heat and stir with a spoon or heatproof rubber spatula until the mixture begins to thicken slightly into a very light, silky custard (a thermometer should read about 76°C/170°F). Keep a close eye on it while you are stirring so you do not allow it to overheat and bubble, or the eggs will scramble. Remove from the heat, immediately pour in the cream and mix again to incorporate. Allow the mixture to cool down.

Pour the mixture into the moulds, leaving a little space at the top.

Freeze until slushy, 60–90 minutes, then insert the sticks and freeze until solid, at least 5 hours or overnight. (See page 22 for the complete procedure.)

PORT & POACHED PEAR

Pear, cinnamon, cloves, peppercorns, ginger, port

Makes 8–10

Luxurious and smooth, pears engulfed in port are often associated with winter, but in poptail form they're so refreshing you can serve them any time of the day or year. There's a whole culture around port drinking, whether it's aristocrats who like it at the end of their formal dinner or rock-and-rollers who like a cheap thrill. Be it an expensive bottle or cheap, it's stronger and more complex than wine, and this poptail with cream drizzled into the moulds makes for a really sumptuous experience.

175ml/¾ cup port
60ml/¼ cup water
150g/¾ cup granulated
  sugar
1 cinnamon stick
2 strips of pared lemon
  zest
4 cloves
8 peppercorns
1.25-cm/½-inch piece of
  ginger, peeled and cut
  into 3 thin slices
750g/1lb 10oz pears,
  peeled, cored and
  chopped (about
  510g/1lb 2oz prepared
  weight)
3–4 tablespoons freshly
  squeezed lemon juice
  (from about 1–2 lemons)
60ml/¼ cup double
  (heavy) cream (optional)

For the garnish (optional):
long-stemmed pear leaf
  for each

Put the port, water, sugar, cinnamon, lemon zest, cloves, peppercorns, ginger and pears into a medium saucepan. Bring to the boil, then reduce to a simmer until the pears are tender, about 15–20 minutes, depending on their ripeness.

Fish the pears out with a slotted spoon, leaving the spices and zest in the pan, and set the pears aside in a bowl. Continue to simmer the port mixture until it is reduced a little; you should have about 240ml/1 cup liquid left.

Strain the liquid through a sieve, over the pears. Purée the mixture in a food processor, then add the lemon juice to taste.

If you like, drizzle about a teaspoon of cream into the bottom of each mould before you pour the mixture into the moulds, leaving a little space at the top. If you like, drop a pear leaf into each.

Freeze until slushy, 60–90 minutes, then insert the sticks and freeze until solid, at least 5 hours or overnight. (See page 22 for the complete procedure.)

SAUTERNES, ALMOND & ORANGE BLOSSOM DREAM

Sauternes, cream, almond, orange blossom water

Makes 8–10

The combination of Sauternes and cream is unexpected and very delicate. Sauternes is made from grapes that have been affected by noble rot, which causes the taste to become partially raisined. The cornflour (cornstarch) gives the poptail a smooth, seductive texture, and also stops the mixture from curdling, while the almond extract and orange blossom take this perfumed pop outdoors for a little sunshine. Sauternes is a wine you should have fun with!

350ml/1½ cups whole milk
1¾ tablespoons cornflour (cornstarch)
250ml/1 cup double (heavy) cream
90g/scant ½ cup granulated sugar
250ml/1 cup Sauternes (or other dessert wine)
½ teaspoon almond extract
2 teaspoons orange blossom water
30g/1oz thinly sliced blanched almonds (optional)

For the garnish (optional):
tiny flower blossoms or chopped almonds

Put 4 tablespoons of the milk in a bowl and mix in the cornflour (cornstarch) to form a smooth paste. Put the remaining milk, cream and sugar in a medium saucepan and heat until just about to simmer, then stir in the cornflour paste. The mixture will thicken. Keep stirring, pour in the Sauternes or dessert wine and stir until the mixture bubbles again, then remove from the heat.

Pour the mixture into a bowl, stir in the almond extract and orange blossom water and allow it to cool. Stir in the sliced blanched almonds, if using.

Pour the mixture into the moulds, leaving a little space at the top. If you like, drop in a flower blossom or some chopped almonds.

Freeze until slushy, 60–90 minutes, then insert the sticks and freeze until solid, at least 5 hours or overnight. (See page 22 for the complete procedure.)

BLOODY RUSSIAN MARTINI

Beetroot, apple, lime, ginger, vodka

Makes 8–10

Ruby-coloured, sweet and earthy, beetroot (beet) is supposed to be a natural aphrodisiac. Enjoy this poptail with a shot of vodka; it will make your lips blood red and ready for kissing.

475ml/2 cups freshly juiced or storebought beetroot (beet) juice
1 teaspoon freshly grated ginger
250ml/1 cup pressed apple juice
2 tablespoons freshly squeezed lime juice
60ml/¼ cup vodka
2 tablespoons sugar, or to taste

For the garnish (optional):
sliver of apple for each

Put all the ingredients into a bowl and stir until blended.

Pour the mixture into the moulds, leaving a little space at the top. If you like, drop a sliver of apple into the top of each.

Freeze until slushy, 60–90 minutes, then insert the sticks and freeze until solid, at least 5 hours or overnight. (See page 22 for the complete procedure.)

BLOODY MARY

Tomato, celery, olives, spices, vodka

Makes 8–10

This savoury "morning after" poptail is a healthy restorative that can be all dressed up with multiple garnishes and snack tidbits, becoming a feast in itself.

40g/1½oz celery, finely chopped;
2 tablespoons sugar; 8 olives,
chopped; 25g/1oz cornichons,
finely chopped, plus 2 tablespoons
of the brine; 60ml/¼ cup vodka;
400ml/1¾ cups tomato juice;
2 tablespoons freshly squeezed lemon juice;
2 teaspoons Worcestershire sauce;

¼ teaspoon Tabasco sauce;
salt and pepper

For the garnishes (optional):
olives, bacon, cucumber, celery,
hot peppers, baby tomatoes,
cornichons, salami, cheese, prawns
(shrimp), dill pickles, pickled onions,
capers, lemon wedges…

Put the celery, sugar, olives, cornichons and brine in a medium bowl
with the vodka. Set aside for 30 minutes, then stir in the tomato juice,
lemon juice, Worcestershire sauce, Tabasco sauce, salt (if needed) and pepper.

Spoon the mixture into the moulds, making sure you divide the ingredients evenly, leaving a
little space at the top.

Freeze until slushy, 60–90 minutes, then insert the sticks, or cocktail skewers (if planning
on serving with garnishes), and freeze until solid, at least 5 hours or overnight. (See page
22 for the complete procedure.)

Serve with your garnishes of choice, if you like.

INDEX

ACKNOWLEDGMENTS

Thank you, Quadrille, for encouraging us to be as creative as we wanted: Helen, for keeping us in line and for your perceptive eye, and Céline for your editing and hand modelling. Pete, thanks for nailing the design of the book. Louise and Alex, for your magical photography and styling – you captured the mood and story of each poptail and it was such a pleasure working with you. Claudia, for your advice, your love and your endless support and encouragement. Paul, for your very big heart – you're always there for us in an emergency. Simon, Ros, Anna and Clive for your constant loving support. Peggy, for your never-ending confidence, Ruth, for your guidance, Nicole, for your special devotion, and Laurie, for your magic and your magic garden. Our agents, Lizzy and Harriet, for looking after us so well. Terry, for your special humour, for reading the drafts, and for trying every single poptail even though you don't normally drink. Most of all, thank you, Lily, for your boundless and joyful enthusiasm – you make the world rock!

Publishing director Sarah Lavelle
Creative director Helen Lewis
Commissioning editor Céline Hughes
Designer Peter Roden
Photographer Louise Hagger
Prop stylist Alexander Breeze
Visual inspiration Nadia Roden
Production Tom Moore, Vincent Smith

First published in 2017 by
Quadrille Publishing
Pentagon House,
52–54 Southwark Street,
London SE1 1UN

Quadrille Publishing is an
imprint of Hardie Grant
www.hardiegrant.com.au

www.quadrille.co.uk
www.quadrille.com

Text © Nadia and Cesar Roden 2017
Photography © Louise Hagger 2017
Illustrations © Peter Roden 2017
Design and layout © 2017 Quadrille
Publishing

Cataloguing in Publication Data: a catalogue record for this book is available from the British Library.

ISBN: 978 184949 958 3

Printed in China